THE GIPPS STREET GANG

MARGARET McALISTER

illustrated by Tamsin Edwards-Francis

Contents

Chapter One
Joining the gang   1

Chapter Two
The secret   6

Chapter Three
The second robbery   13

Chapter Four
Disaster   19

Chapter Five
Arrested   24

Chapter Six
The gang   30

Chapter Seven
Uncle Max   36

Chapter One

Joining the gang

When he first moved to the new house in Gipps Street, Collie had no friends. For a while he was lonely.

Then he met the Gipps Street Gang. There were three of them — Rory, Kate and Jack. Collie started riding to school with them.

But one thing spoiled it. Sometimes they went away without him. They would be gone for hours. Then they would come riding back fast. They would all run into Jack's house. They had a secret.

Collie felt left out.

He tried everything he knew to get Jack to ask him to join the gang. He didn't like Jack much, but Jack was the leader. It was better to put up with Jack than have no friends. So he did whatever Jack dared him to do. Even if he got into trouble for it.

Then one day, Jack came to his house after school.

"All right, Collie dog," he said. "I know you want to join the gang, don't you?"

Collie hated it when Jack called him Collie dog.

"I guess so," he said.

"You have to swear to keep our secrets," said Jack, looking mean. "Okay?"

"Okay," said Collie.

"And you have to prove you're good enough," said Jack. He laughed.

Collie's heart banged hard against his chest. What were they going to make him do?

Chapter Two

The secret

The secret was bad. Really bad.
 The gang stole stuff. To join the gang, he had to steal three things. He felt dizzy. He wished he was safe back at his old house.

"You're chicken," said Jack. "I can see it."

"I'm not," said Collie. He looked away from Jack's cold brown eyes. Just three things. Then he would be in the gang. Then he could stop. "I'll do it," he said.

"Good," said Jack. "You can do the first shop today."

Collie felt his insides turn to jelly.

"Today?"

"Yeah, today." Jack went to the door. "Or you don't get into the gang."

So Collie went with them. To the biggest store in the mall.

"Go in and nick a wallet," said Jack. "We'll wait outside."

There was a cardboard policeman near the entry. A sign on it said "Shopstealing is a crime". Collie felt sicker than ever. He would end up in jail. His mother would cry. His father would yell. What would Uncle Max think? Uncle Max had his own shop. He hated shopstealers.

Collie walked around the store about six times. Then he did it. He took a quick look around. He grabbed a wallet from the shelf and pushed it in his pocket.

He didn't want to walk past the lady at the door. What if she asked to check his pockets? He picked up a fluffy toy. He paid for it at the checkout.

He walked out.

Nobody stopped him. Nobody knew.

The others jumped up as soon as they saw him. Jack grabbed the bag. He pulled out the fluffy rabbit. "What's THIS?"

"It was just so they wouldn't suspect me," said Collie. His face felt hot. "Let's get out of here."

"Where's the wallet?" asked Jack.

"Here. See?" Collie took the wallet out of his pocket. It was an ugly thing. It was cheap and brown.

"All right." Jack gave an evil smile. "Let's go."

Chapter Three

The second robbery

The Gipps Street Gang had a whole box of stuff. It was in Jack's cupboard. They didn't use any of it.

"I don't get it," Collie said. "Why do you steal it? If you don't want it?"

"For fun," said Jack. "To show we're smarter than they are." He stuck his face up close to Collie's. "You got a problem with that?"

"No problem," said Collie. Jack scared him. Now that Collie knew their secret, Jack would never leave him alone.

"Good. Tomorrow you hit the games shop," said Jack. "That little shop near the doughnut place."

Collie stared at him. "The games shop?"

"Yeah. It's harder. The bloke in there watches you."

After that, Collie got away as soon as he could. He didn't eat any dinner. His mother kept asking him if he was sick. He was, in a way. Sick with fear. Sick with shame.

The games shop was his Uncle Max's place. They were asking him to rob his own uncle.

The next day, the gang stayed outside again. He walked into the store.

"Well, hello!" said Uncle Max. "How's my favourite nephew? Do you like your new house?"

"Not really," said Collie. "I wish we'd never moved."

"Yeah, it's hard making new friends. But I've got something here that might cheer you up."

"What?" asked Collie miserably.

"It's a new wizard," said Uncle Max. "For your collection. See?" He walked over to the shelf and picked up the wizard. It was beautiful. It held a swirly, glowing blue globe in its hands.

"Wow!" Collie took it gently. "It's great."

"I'll wrap it up for you." His uncle walked away. Quickly, Collie picked up a small game and put it in his pocket. He hated doing it. He felt bad.

"Uncle Max?"

"Yes, mate?"

"Would you mind keeping the wizard for me for a while? I'm going riding with friends."

"No problem." Uncle Max looked at Collie. "Are you feeling all right? You look a bit sick."

"I'm okay. But I've got to go. Thanks for the wizard, Uncle Max."

His Uncle smiled at him. "Good to see you. Come back soon!"

Collie walked out with his head down. If Uncle Max knew he was a thief, he'd never want to talk to him again.

Chapter Four

Disaster

It was Saturday morning. He and the gang were standing outside a big clothing store.

"The last thing," said Jack. "You have to nick a T-shirt. Or do you want to chicken out?"

Collie felt angry. "No," he said. He hated Jack.

He went into the shop. He was carrying a bag of fruit.

He walked up to a rack of T-shirts. He looked around. No-one was near him. He took a red T-shirt. He looked around again. Quickly he pushed it in under the fruit.

He walked out of the shop. The girl at the door asked to check his bag. He held it open so she could see the fruit.

"Okay," she said.

He was free!

He went towards the gang. Then he felt a hand on his arm.

"Not so fast, young man," said a voice.

A tall man frowned down at him. His heart started banging hard in his chest.

"I think you may have forgotten to pay for some goods," said the man. "You'd better come with me."

Collie looked at the gang. Jack made a horrible face and put his finger on his lips.

"Come on," said the man again. He held Collie's arm tighter. "Back into the shop."

People were watching. This was the most awful thing that had ever happened to him. He put his head down. His face was burning hot. He went back into the shop.

Chapter Five

Arrested

The manager was angry. "You're just a common thief," he said. "A criminal. It costs me money every time people like you steal. Then I have to put prices up for everyone else."

Collie didn't want to cry, but he couldn't help it. The man who had caught him was writing. It was a report for the police — all about how he saw Collie stealing.

"The police will be here soon," said the manager. "You'll have to go to the police station. What are your parents going to say?"

"I don't know," said Collie. He wanted to hide.

When the police came, they didn't look at all friendly. He looked at their blue uniforms and black belts. Big tears slid down his nose.

He had to walk out of the shop between two policemen.

More people stared and whispered. He had to get into the back of the police car. He put his hands over his face.

At the police station, they rang his parents. His dad came in his old T-shirt and gardening shorts. He looked upset. And angry. Collie had to tell him about stealing the T-shirt.

Before he could go home, Collie had to answer lots more questions. How much money did he have? Why did he take the T-shirt? Had he taken anything else? It was awful.

Collie said nothing about the gang. He knew what Jack's finger across his lips had meant. *Don't tell. Or else.*

Chapter Six

The gang

His parents didn't understand. Why did he have to steal? Why did he do it? He couldn't tell them. He couldn't tell anyone. How could he say, "Because Jack said I had to"?

He had to stay in all weekend. On Monday, the others were waiting at the corner. Jack stepped up close. "Did you tell them about the gang?" he said. He grabbed Collie's shirt. "You'd better not have, or you'll be dead meat."

"I didn't say anything," said Collie.

"Okay then," said Jack. "You'd better try a different shop next time. They'll be watching you now."

"Next time?" Collie looked at him. Then he knew. Jack wasn't going to stop. To stay in the gang, Collie would have to *keep* stealing.

"I can't," said Collie. "I'm grounded. For two weeks."

"So? You can sneak out. Or are you just chicken?" Jack pushed Collie so his bike fell sideways. "Chicken, chicken, chicken!"

Collie got mad. He threw his bike on the ground. He ran at Jack and hit him.

"Get him!" shouted Jack, swinging back at him. "Rory, get him!"

"You're so dumb!" yelled Collie. His fist hit Jack on the nose. "You're all stupid! And your *gang's* stupid!"

Kate screamed. Rory backed off.

Jack's nose was bleeding. He swore. "I'll get you for this, Collie," he said. "You just wait."

"You do," said Collie, "and I'll tell everything. See how you like going to the police station."

He was still scared. But it felt good to tell Jack what he thought of him. It felt good not to do what Jack said any more.

Jack swore again. "I'll get you. You'll see." He got on his bike and rode away.

Rory and Kate stood there.

"I'm sorry you got caught, Collie," said Kate.

"Yeah," said Collie. He still felt angry with her. With the whole gang.

"You won't really tell on us, will you?" she said.

"Oh, shut up," said Collie.

"It was all Jack's idea," said Rory.

Collie didn't want to talk to them any more. He got on his bike and went.

Chapter Seven

Uncle Max

On Tuesday night Uncle Max came to visit.

"Hello, Collie," he said. "I brought your wizard over."

Collie went red. He looked at the beautiful wizard. "I can't take it," he said.

"And why is that, Collie?" His uncle looked puzzled.

"Because . . ." Collie couldn't speak. How could he tell his uncle? But he had to. He felt sick with shame.

"I took something," he said.

"Took something?" said his uncle. "What do you mean?"

Collie told him. All about the Gipps Street Gang. About the box of loot. About the little game he had taken.

"I know you'll hate me," said Collie. "A *shopstealer.*"

"Poor Collie." His uncle's voice was sad, but kind. "You learned your lesson the hard way, didn't you?"

"You don't have to be nice to me," said Collie.

"And why wouldn't I?"

"I'm sorry I took the game," said Collie. "I'll pay you for it."

"No," said Uncle Max. "Do me a favour instead. Work for me on Thursday nights and Saturday mornings. That's the worst time for shopstealers. You can help spot them."

Collie sat up straight. He felt a bit better. "Okay," he said. "Why don't we get one of those cardboard policemen to stand in the corner?"

"You think that's a good idea?" asked Uncle Max.

Collie thought of the policemen who came to get him. The blue uniforms. The police car. Every time he looked at that cardboard policeman it gave him the shivers.

"It's a great idea," he said. "Trust me!"

"I trust you," said Uncle Max. He smiled. "You'll always be my favourite nephew."